PORTRAITS OF THE STATES

UTAH

by Jonatha A. Brown

Please visit our web site at: www.garethstevens.com
For a free color catalog describing Gareth Stevens Publishing's list of high-quality books and multimedia programs, call 1-800-542-2595 (USA) or 1-800-387-3178 (Canada).
Gareth Stevens Publishing's fax: (414) 332-3567.

Library of Congress Cataloging-in-Publication Data

Brown, Jonatha A.
Utah / Jonatha A. Brown.
p. cm. — (Portraits of the states)
Includes bibliographical references and index.
ISBN-10: 0-8368-4709-1 — ISBN-13: 978-0-8368-4709-3 (lib. bdg.)
ISBN-10: 0-8368-4726-1 — ISBN-13: 978-0-8368-4726-0 (softcover)
1. Utah—Juvenile literature. I. Title. II. Series.
F826.3.B76 2007
979.2—dc22 2005036641

This edition first published in 2007 by
Gareth Stevens Publishing
A Member of the WRC Media Family of Companies
330 West Olive Street, Suite 100
Milwaukee, WI 53212 USA

Editorial direction: Mark J. Sachner
Project manager: Jonatha A. Brown
Editor: Catherine Gardner
Art direction and design: Tammy West
Picture research: Diane Laska-Swanke
Indexer: Walter Kronenberg
Production: Jessica Morris and Robert Kraus

Picture credits: Cover, pp. 4, 18, 25, 27, 28 © John Elk III; p. 5 © Robert Lindholm/Visuals Unlimited; pp. 6, 21, 26 © Tom Bean; p. 9 © Otto Herschan/Getty Images; p. 10 © Hulton Archive/Getty Images; p. 11 © Jonathan Blair/CORBIS; p. 12 © Lee Cohen/CORBIS; pp. 15, 24 © Gibson Stock Photography; p. 16 © Myrleen Ferguson Cate/PhotoEdit; p. 22 © Bill Ross/CORBIS; p. 29 © AP Images

Printed in the United States of America

1 2 3 4 5 6 7 8 9 10 09 08 07 06

CONTENTS

Words that are defined in the Glossary appear in **bold** the first time they are used in the text.

On the Cover: Bryce Canyon National Park is a wonderful place to go hiking. The rocky forms in the canyon are sure to amaze you.

Introduction

If you could visit Utah, what would you like to do? Would you visit Dinosaur National Monument? There, you could see the bones of huge beasts that roamed the Earth long ago. Would you head for the mountains to ski? Utah has awesome ski resorts. You could even take lessons at the Utah Olympic Park!

This state is beautiful. It has mountains, deserts, steep canyons, and rugged rocky landscapes. It has cliff dwellings built by Native people hundreds of years ago, too. In fact, Utah has more beauty, history, and adventure than you could possibly take in during just one trip.

So, come to Utah! It is a wonderful place to explore.

The rock towers of Castle Valley rise high above the Colorado River valley.

The state flag of Utah.

UTAH FACTS

- Became the 45th U.S. State: January 4, 1896
- Population (2004): 2,389,039
- Capital: Salt Lake City
- Biggest Cities: Salt Lake City, West Valley City, Provo, Sandy City
- Size: 82,144 square miles (212,753 square kilometers)
- Nickname: The Beehive State
- State Tree: Blue spruce
- State Flower: Sego lily
- State Animal: Rocky Mountain elk
- State Bird: California gull

History

Native Americans have lived in Utah for thousands of years. By the 1300s, several different tribes lived there. They included the Ute, Shoshone, Navajo, and Paiute people.

White Explorers and Trappers

The first white men reached the Utah area in 1776. Silvestre Vélez de Escalante and Francisco Atanasio Dominguez were from Spain. The Spanish claimed the land, but they did not try to build towns there.

Spain also held Mexico at this time. In 1821, Mexico broke away from Spain and took control of Utah. Yet Mexicans did not try to settle this region.

American fur trappers moved to the area in the 1820s. They found plenty of beaver. They trapped the beaver and sold their **pelts**. Within a few years, most of the beaver there had been caught, so the trappers left.

Long ago, Native people built homes in the cliffs of Utah. This old cliff dwelling can be seen at Grand Staircase-Escalante National Monument.

IN UTAH S HISTORY

The Anasazi

The Anasazi came to southeastern Utah about two thousand years ago. They wove baskets, grew squash and corn, and raised turkeys. They built houses high above the ground, in the faces of cliffs. The Anasazi left this area in about 1300. The remains of their cliff houses can still be seen in southern Utah today.

A New Church

At about this time, a new kind of Christian church was founded in New York. It was the Church of Jesus Christ of Latter-day Saints. Members of this church, called Mormons, took their faith very seriously. They formed close groups and stayed away from people of other faiths.

Many people disliked the Mormons. One reason was that Mormon men often had more than one wife. This is called **polygamy**. Most other people at that time thought polygamy was wrong. Some of them hurt Mormons or broke into their churches and ruined them.

To get away from the bad treatment and hatred, the Mormons moved to Illinois. There, their leader was killed by an angry crowd in 1844. Then, a man named Brigham Young took over as the head of the church. He wanted to take the Mormons to a safe

IN UTAH S HISTORY

Mountain Men

The early white trappers were called "mountain men." Jim Bridger was a mountain man. He was said to know the land in Utah better than anyone. He became a scout and led many groups of people across this land. Jedediah Smith was famous, too. He was the first white man to travel west from Utah to California. These were just two of the many mountain men who blazed new trails in Utah.

place. Young chose a spot that was outside the United States. Few people lived in this area. It seemed to be land no one else wanted. This land was in Utah.

Early Mormon Settlement

The first Mormons arrived in Salt Lake Valley in 1847. The area was dry and dusty, but the Mormons had big plans for it. They **irrigated** the land so they could grow crops. They also built Salt Lake City.

Thousands of Mormons came to the new city. They built other towns nearby.

In 1848, the United States and Mexico signed a **treaty**. This treaty gave the land in Utah to the United States. The U.S. Congress created the **Territory** of Utah two years later. Brigham Young was its first governor.

Saved by Birds

In 1848, huge swarms of crickets attacked the crops in Utah. Luckily, big flocks of gulls arrived and ate the crickets. The gulls saved the crops and saved the settlers lives. Many years later, the California gull was named the state bird of Utah.

The Utah War

Problems soon arose. The U.S. government did not want men to take more than one wife. The Mormons felt differently. They wanted to live in their own way.

In 1857, the Utah War began. The Mormons of Utah fought the U.S. Army. The next year, the Mormons lost. They agreed to accept a governor for the territory who was not a Mormon.

This Shoshone family was photographed in Salt Lake City in 1860. A few years later, their tribe was forced to move to a reservation.

Big Changes

In the 1860s, some changes came to Utah. The first was a telegraph line that ran all the way from the East Coast to the West Coast. In Salt Lake City, the two halves of the telegraph line met. This line connected Utah to the rest of the country.

Another change was a new railroad that ran across the country. The final spike of the rail line was driven into the tracks in Utah. Trains soon made travel to and from Utah much easier than it had been.

In the late 1860s, silver and gold were discovered in Utah's mountains. Lead, copper, and coal also were

IN UTAH'S HISTORY

Fighting with Natives

As more white people moved to Utah, the Natives in the area grew angry. In the 1850s and 1860s, the Natives tried to drive the Mormons away. The most famous conflict was known as the Black Hawk War. It took place in the mid-1860s. In the end, the Natives lost. They were forced to move to **reservations**.

found. These rich mineral deposits drew miners and other settlers to the Utah Territory. Few of the new people were Mormons.

The people of Utah wanted their territory to become a state. The U.S. Congress did not agree. It did not want a state that allowed polygamy. During the 1880s, Congress passed laws to take rights away from men with more than one wife. These men had to pay fines, too. Other laws took property away from the Mormon Church. Finally, the leader of the church gave in. He asked the Mormons to give up polygamy. Utah became a state on January 4, 1896.

FUN FACTS

A Long Wait to Become a State

The people of Utah asked to become a state seven times before the U.S. Congress agreed. They asked the first time in 1850. It took forty-six years for the Congress and the people of the state to agree on the terms for Utah to be a state!

The railroad linked Salt Lake City to the east and west coasts. It helped the city grow.

Famous People of Utah

Butch Cassidy

Born: April 15, 1866, Circleville, Utah

Died: about 1910, Bolivia, South America

Butch Cassidy was born Robert Leroy Parker. He grew up to be a famous outlaw. When he was a boy, Cassidy started stealing cattle. Later, he joined a gang that **rustled** cattle and horses and robbed banks and trains. In 1900, Cassidy teamed up with a man called the Sundance Kid. With the police chasing them, they escaped to South America. No one is sure when Cassidy died, but one story says he and "the Kid" were shot by police in Bolivia in about 1910.

Good and Bad Times

The new state grew. Mining was the main **industry** there. Farming and ranching were important, too. Irrigation helped people grow crops for themselves and grass for cattle. Factories were built in the cities.

Prices for goods fell all over the country in the 1930s. In Utah, factories and mines closed. Workers lost their jobs. This period in history was known as the **Great Depression**.

A **drought** hit Utah, too. Without enough rain, crops died. Some farmers gave up and left the state.

During the early 1940s, the United States began fighting in World War II. Army bases were set up in Utah. Farmers there grew food for the soldiers. Utah

The 2002 Winter Olympic Games brought huge crowds and plenty of excitement to Salt Lake City.

miners mined metal ore, and factories made goods to help fight the war. These changes brought jobs back to Utah.

Utah Today

Since the war, the state has continued to grow. Now, factories provide more jobs in Utah than farming and mining. **Tourism** is another important industry.

In 2002, Salt Lake City hosted the Winter Olympic Games. This huge event brought many visitors to the state.

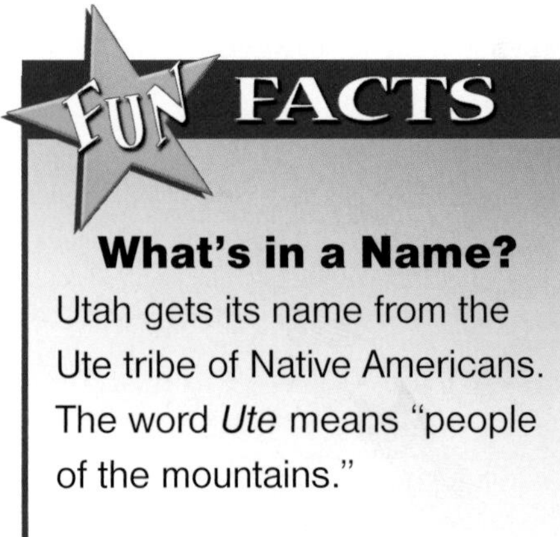

What's in a Name?

Utah gets its name from the Ute tribe of Native Americans. The word *Ute* means "people of the mountains."

Time Line

1300s	The Anasazi leave the Utah area, and other Native tribes move in.
1776	Silvestre Vélez de Escalante and Francisco Atanasio Dominguez claim this area for Spain.
1820s	White trappers begin moving into the area.
1847	Mormons begin settling in Salt Lake City.
1848	The United States gains control of Utah.
1857-1858	Mormons fight U.S. soldiers in the Utah War.
1896	Utah becomes the forty-fifth U.S. state.
1929	The Great Depression begins, and many miners lose their jobs.
1931	A drought hits Utah and causes many farmers to go broke.
1941	The United States enters World War II. Factories in Utah hire workers to help make supplies for the war effort.
1960	Tourism begins to grow in Utah.
2002	Salt Lake City hosts the Winter Olympic Games.

People

More than two million people live in Utah. The state is growing fast. Between 1990 and 2000, its **population** grew by nearly 30 percent. This makes Utah the fourth fastest-growing state in the nation.

Almost 90 percent of all Utahns live in or near cities. Few people live in the country. Salt Lake City is the largest city in Utah. It is in the northern part of the state. This area is known as the Wasatch Front. Almost all of the state's big cities

Hispanics

This chart shows the different racial backgrounds of people in Utah. In the 2000 U.S. Census, 9 percent of the people who live in Utah called themselves Latino or Hispanic. Most of them or their relatives came from places where Spanish is spoken. Hispanics do not appear on this chart because they may come from any racial background.

The People of Utah

Total Population 2,389,039

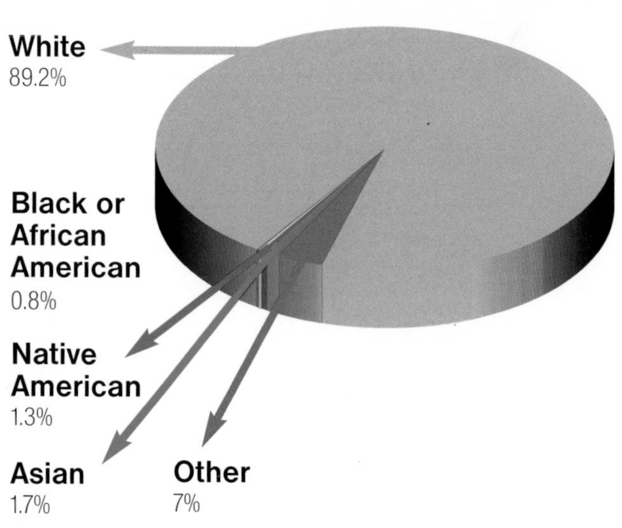

Percentages are based on the 2000 Census.

Salt Lake City is the largest city in Utah and the state's business center. This city is the international center for the Mormon religion, too.

are found there. Most of these big cities lie within 50 miles (80 km) of Salt Lake City.

Where People Come from

Nearly nine out of every ten Utahns can trace the roots of their families back to places in Europe. Many of them have **ancestors** who came from Britain. Other Utah families can trace their roots to Germany, Denmark, Sweden, and Ireland.

In Utah, 9 percent of the people are Hispanic. Most of these people came from Mexico. Others came from Central and South America. Some of these **immigrants** can speak both Spanish and English. Others can speak only Spanish.

In recent years, the state's Asian population has grown.

A marching band plays to a huge crowd during a football game at Brigham Young University.

Many people have moved to Utah from countries such as Vietnam, China, and Japan.

Meanwhile, the number of Native Americans has been shrinking. Most Natives live on one of eight reservations in the state. The Uintah and Ouray Reservation is one of the largest of them. It is in northern Utah.

Religion

Today, nearly three-fourths of the people in Utah are Mormons. Salt Lake City is the center of their religion. The huge Salt Lake Temple was built there in 1893. Mormons often have large families. As a result, Utah has the highest birth rate of any state in the country.

The next largest religious groups are Roman Catholics

and Protestants. Buddhists, Jews, and Muslims can be found in Utah, as well.

Schools Then and Now

Education has long been important to the Mormons. They opened schools when they arrived here in 1847. Even so, public schools were not set up in the state until 1890. That year, laws were passed to create free grade schools for all. Five years later, the first public high schools opened.

The state has ten public colleges and universities. The University of Utah is the largest of them. It has about 27,500 students. It is located in Salt Lake City. Among private colleges and universities in Utah, the best-known is Brigham Young University. It is in Provo.

Famous People of Utah

Martha Hughes Cannon

Born: 1857, Llandudno, Wales

Died: July 10, 1932, Los Angeles, California

Martha Hughes Cannon was an amazing person. As a child, she made the trip to Utah in a covered wagon. When she was fourteen years old, she started teaching school. Later, Cannon went to college, but she did not behave like most women of her time. Instead, she cut her hair short and wore men's boots. Then, she became a doctor in Salt Lake City. She opened the first nursing school in the city. Cannon entered politics in 1896. She ran against her husband for a seat on the Utah State Senate and won! This made Martha Hughes Cannon the first woman ever to serve as a state senator in the United States.

The Land

Utah is in the western United States. Mountains and deserts cover most of the land here. Utah is a rugged place.

The Rocky Mountains

The northeastern part of Utah is in the Rocky Mountains. "The Rockies" run through several western states and include many mountain ranges. Two of these ranges lie in Utah. The Wasatch Range runs from north to south near the middle of the state. The Uinta Range lies farther east. Unlike most ranges in the Rockies, it runs from east to west. The state's highest point is found in this part of the state. This point is Kings Peak. It is 13,528 feet (4,123 meters) above sea level.

FUN FACTS

Four Corners

At its southeastern corner, Utah touches the borders of three other states. They are Arizona, Colorado, and New Mexico. This is the only place in the country where four states meet. It is called the Four Corners.

In the fall, trees in the Wasatch Mountains put on a colorful display.

UTAH

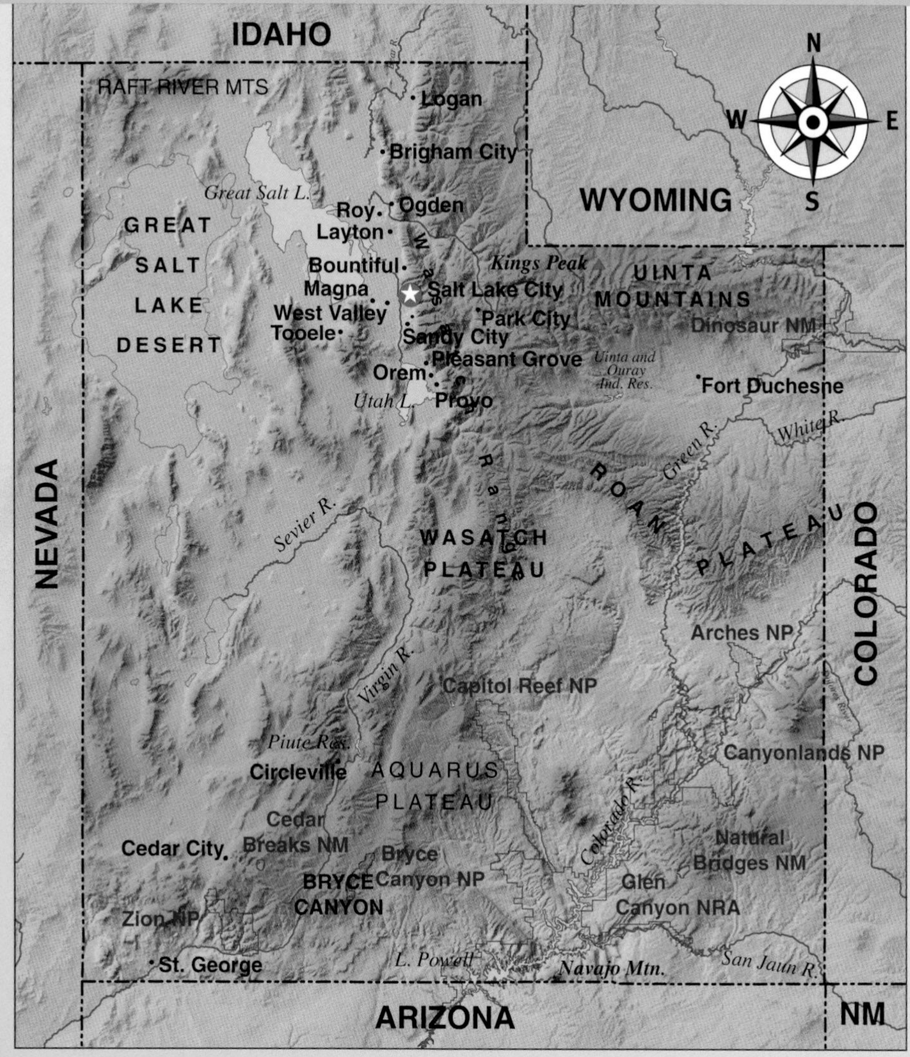

This region gets plenty of snow and rain. Pine, sycamore, and aspen trees grow in the forests. Wildflowers and grasses grow here, as well. This wild place is home to black bears, cougars, mountain goats, elk, and moose.

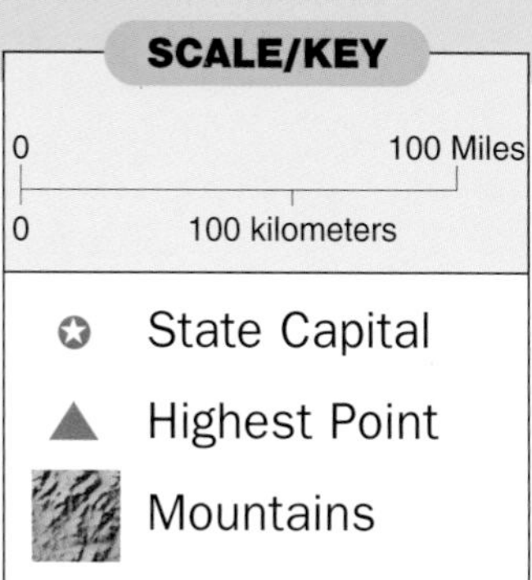

The Great Basin

In the western third of the state is a desert region called the Great Basin. It is made up of craggy mountains and wide valleys. Salt lakes once covered the valleys. Today, only dirt and salt remain. In some places, the salt makes the land look white.

The Great Basin gets little rain. Joshua and mesquite trees grow here, along with cactuses. Coyotes, snakes, and lizards are at home in this region. Jackrabbits, mice and prairie dogs are often seen.

The best soil in the state is found in this region. It is in a narrow strip between the Great Salt Lake and the Wasatch Mountains. Most of Utah's people live here.

The Colorado Plateau

The Colorado Plateau lies in the southeast. Over millions of years, rivers have cut deep gorges through this part of the state. Many strange and rocky forms can be found here. They include towers, ridges, and arches. There also are steep-sided hills known as **buttes** and big flat-topped areas called **mesas**. In this part of the state, sandstone is the main rock. In different places, the stone is yellow, pink, white, red, and brown.

Like the Great Basin, the Colorado Plateau is a dry area. It is much warmer than the mountains of the northeastern part of Utah.

Major Rivers

Colorado River
1,450 miles (2,334 km) long

Green River
730 miles (1,175 km) long

Sevier River
279 miles (449 km) long

Waterways

One body of water stands out more than any of the others in Utah. It is the Great Salt Lake. This is the largest saltwater lake in North America.

The other big lakes here contain freshwater. Utah Lake is the largest of the freshwater lakes. Lake Powell is a big man-made lake. It was created when a dam was built on the Colorado River.

The Colorado River is the longest river in Utah. Many other rivers flow into it. The Colorado River drains much of the land in the southeastern part of Utah.

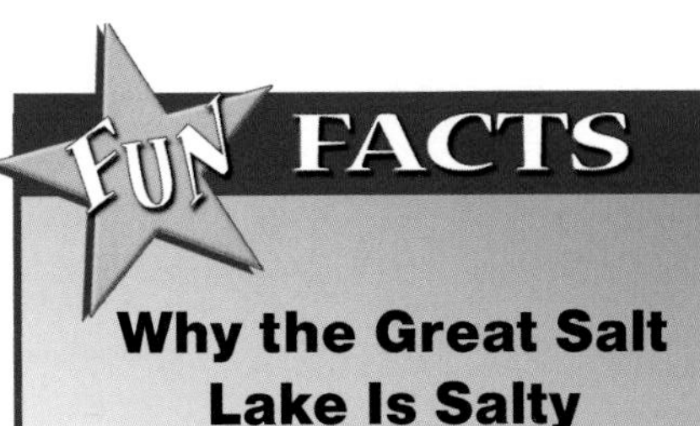

Why the Great Salt Lake Is Salty

The Great Salt Lake is much saltier than an ocean. Rivers flow into this huge lake. They carry salt and other minerals. But no rivers flow out of the lake. Instead, some of the water in the lake dries up in the warm, dry air. Minerals are left behind. The Great Salt Lake gets saltier and saltier every year.

The Great Salt Lake is much saltier than the ocean. Fish cannot live in this salty water.

Economy

Long ago, most Utahns were farmers and miners. Now, far more people work in offices than on the land.

Many people in Utah work in service jobs. Service workers help other people. Doctors, nurses, and teachers are service workers. Car mechanics, lawyers, and bankers provide services, too.

Tourism is a growing business in this state. Tourists come here to ski and to visit national parks. They stay in hotels and eat in restaurants. These places hire workers to serve the tourists. Tourism creates many service jobs.

Making Goods

Factories provide jobs for the people of Utah, too. Some factory workers make

Utah is a great place to ski! Every winter, thousands of skiers hit the slopes here.

rocket engines. Others make computers and office machines. Some process the crops and animals raised on the state's farms. They mill flour and package meat and milk products.

Using Natural Resources

The state still has more than fifteen thousand farms. The top farm products are beef cattle, sheep, and pigs. Chickens are becoming an important farm product, too. Only about one-fourth of the farmers in Utah use their land for growing crops. The biggest crops are hay, corn, and wheat.

Some mining still takes place here. The state's main mineral products are oil and natural gas. Coal is also important. Copper, gold, and other metals are mined in Utah as well.

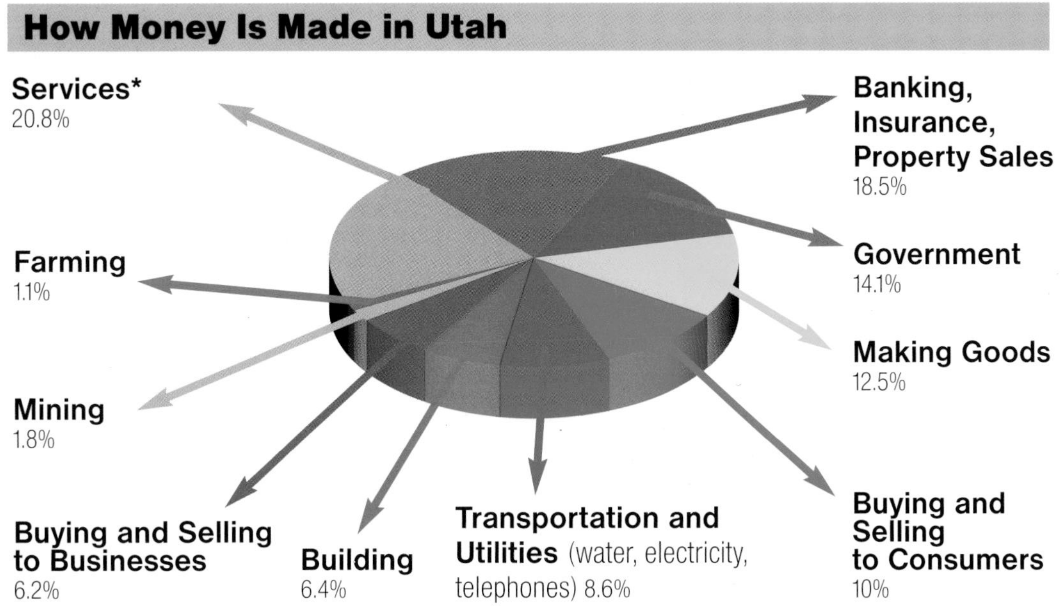

* Services include jobs in hotels, restaurants, car repair, medicine, teaching, and entertainment.

Government

Salt Lake City is the capital of Utah. The leaders of the state work there. The state government has three parts. They are the executive, legislative, and judicial branches.

Executive Branch

The job of the executive branch is to carry out the state's laws. The governor is the head of this branch. The lieutenant governor and other officials help.

Utah's state capitol building is in Salt Lake City. It was built in the early 1900s.

The Governor's Mansion was built in Salt Lake City in 1902. Today, it is a well-known tourist site as well as the home of the governor of Utah.

Legislative Branch

The Utah legislature makes the laws for the state. It has two parts. The parts are the House of Representatives and the Senate. These two groups work together.

Judicial Branch

Judges and courts make up the judicial branch. Judges and courts may decide whether people who have been **accused of** committing crimes are guilty.

Local Government

The state has twenty-nine counties. Most counties are run by a team of three people known as the board of commissioners. Cities are run by a city council and a city manager or mayor.

UTAH'S STATE GOVERNMENT

Executive

Office	Length of Term
Governor	4 years
Lieutenant Governor	4 years

Legislative

Body	Length of Term
Senate (29 members)	4 years
House of Representatives (75 members)	2 years

Judicial

Court	Length of Term
Supreme (5 justices)	10 years
Appeals (7 judges)	6 years

CHAPTER

7

Things to See and Do

Utah is full of things to see and do. Dinosaur National Monument in Jensen has some of the best displays of dinosaur bones in the country. For more recent history, drive along the Trail of the Ancients. You will see cliff dwellings and other **remnants** of the Anasazi.

Salt Lake City

Salt Lake City is the home of the Salt Lake Temple and Mormon Tabernacle. These buildings celebrate the Mormon faith. The Mormon Tabernacle Choir is a famous singing group. It is made up of 320 men and women. They perform

At Dinosaur National Monument, you can see dinosaur bones that are millions of years old.

all over the world, but the home base for the group is the Mormon Tabernacle.

Another interesting stop in Salt Lake City is This Is the Place Heritage Park. It features a rebuilt frontier town where you can learn about the lives of Mormons in the mid-1800s. If you visit in late July, you can enjoy a folk music festival there, too.

Busy as Bees

This state's nickname is the Beehive State. The Mormons who settled here thought of themselves as being like bees: hardworking, steady, and careful. They chose a picture of a beehive to stand for these qualities. A beehive is shown on the state flag and the Great Seal of Utah.

Enjoying the Outdoors

Southern Utah is filled with rocky canyons, arches, and ridges. Some of this land has been set aside in national parks. Each park offers amazing views from roads and hiking trails. Bryce Canyon, Arches, and Zion National Park are a few of these wonderful parks.

You will have lots of fun and adventure

In the evenings, the Salt Lake Temple is a beautiful sight. Many tourists visit this temple in Salt Lake City each year.

Famous People of Utah

Jim Beckwourth

Born: April 26, 1798, Fredericksburg, Virginia

Died: September 25, 1866, Denver, Colorado

James Beckwourth was born a slave. After he was freed by his owner, he headed west and became a mountain man. He lived for years with Native tribes in Utah and other parts of the West. His adventures left him with many tales to tell. Most of the stories featured Beckwourth as the hero. The stories may not have been completely true, but they made him famous.

Arches National Park is home to the Landscape Arch. This arch is thought to be the longest natural arch in the world.

in the Rocky Mountains. In summer, you can hike, fish, and camp. In winter, you can enjoy some of the best skiing in the country. Park City, Deer Valley, and other ski areas await you!

Sports and Festivals

Utah's sports fans are proud of their pro basketball team, the Utah Jazz. The team's home court is in Salt Lake City. College sports are popular, too. Thousands of fans support the football teams at the University of Utah and Brigham Young University.

Festivals are a big part of life in Utah. The Sundance Film Festival takes place in Park City. This event is famous around the world. The Utah Arts Festival is also well known. It draws thousands of art lovers to Salt Lake City each June.

And no trip to Utah is complete without a visit to a real Native American powwow. One of the best-known is the Ute PowWow in Fort Duchesne.

Famous People of Utah

Debbi Fields

Born: September 18, 1956, East Oakland, California

Debbi Fields turned a small shop into a big business. In 1977, she opened a small cookie shop in California. Her cookies were a huge hit, so she opened more shops. In 1982, she moved to Park City. She moved the main office of Mrs. Fields Cookies there, too. Her company now has more than seven hundred stores around the world.

Mehmet Okur scores as he helps the Utah Jazz defeat the Golden State Warriors in a 2006 game.

GLOSSARY

accused of — blamed for

ancestors — members of a family who lived long ago

buttes — flat-topped hills with steep sides

drought — a long period without rain

Great Depression — a time in the 1930s when many people lost their jobs, farmers lost their land, and businesses lost money

immigrants — people who leave one country to live in another country

industry — a group of businesses that offer the same type of service or product

irrigated — brought water to fields through pipes, ditches, and canals

mesas — flat-topped mountains with steep sides

pelts — skins with fur on them

polygamy — being married to two or more husbands or wives

population — the number of people who live in a city, state, or other place

remnants — small parts of things that are left over

reservations — lands set aside by the government for Natives, who were forced to live there

rustled — stole farm or ranch animals

territory — a place that belongs to a country

tourism — the business of helping people who travel for pleasure

treaty — an agreement between two or more people or groups

TO FIND OUT MORE

Books

A Is for Arches: A Utah Alphabet. Discover America State By State (series). Becky Hall (Thomson Gale)

The Colorado River. Rivers of North America (series). Daniel Gilpin (Gareth Stevens)

Utah. This Land Is Your Land (series). Ann Heinrichs (Compass Point Books)

Utah. United States (series). Paul Joseph (Abdo and Daughers)

The Utes. Native Peoples (series). Allison Lassieur (Bridgestone Books)

Web Sites

Bryce Canyon National Park
www.nps.gov/brca/

Dinosaur National Monument
www.desertusa.com/dino/

Enchanted Learning: Utah
www.enchantedlearning.com/usa/states/utah/

Utah Facts
www.teachervision.fen.com/page/8610.html

Utah: History for Kids
historyforkids.utah.gov/fun_and_games/index.html

INDEX